Mystery
Of
Altars and Foundations

Apostle Joshua Selman

Copyright © 2020 www.battlecryng.com All rights reserved

This is a dedicated and passionate project of putting out Sermons of Apostle Joshua Selman to reach more souls and make his messages available beyond borders, and give more people options to partake in the transformation through the word of God, everything in this book is for informative purposes only, it is not intended to cure or treat any ailment.

No part of this book may be reproduced, or stored in a retrieval system, or transmitted in any form or by any means, electronic, mechanical, photocopying, recording, or otherwise, without express written permission of the publisher

For more enquiries:

Contact us at: sales@battlecryng.com

THE MYSTERY OF ALTARS AND FOUNDATIONS

The hallmark of a true apostolic ministry is not just the ability to produce results in the lives of people, it's not just the ability to reveal a dimension of God to a generation, an apostolic ministry's responsibility goes beyond that.

I Peter 2 vs 5: Ye also, as lively stones, are built up a spiritual house, an holy priesthood, to offer up spiritual sacrifices, acceptable to God by Jesus Christ.

In *vs 4* he talks about Christ being the cornerstone, then in vs 5

Ye also, as lively stones, are built up a spiritual house, an holy priesthood, to offer up spiritual sacrifices, acceptable to God by Jesus Christ... that means that the destination of everything that the Holy Spirit is doing through different vessels and ministries is that a single edifice called a spiritual house becomes the result. So, Paul said as a wise master builder, I have laid the foundation and he said another will build on this foundation and he said let every man be careful how he builds, so, an apostolic ministry is not just one that has the experience of the dimensions of God and has had encounters and can bring the bodies to these experiences but one who is like an architect that is building the body in accordance with the requisite proportions of the different components so that, that edifice can be produced and will fit the description in Revelations 21, that the building is a perfect square, the length, the height, the width are equal and we are privileged by grace and election to be part of a ministry that is consciously and consistently doing this, not exaggerating any aspect of the body of Christ or the kingdom above another so that we will not have a loop sided group.

2 Peter 1 vs 3 says According as his divine power hath given unto us all things that [pertain] unto life and godliness,.. he told us expressly that there are things that pertain to life and there are things that pertain to godliness, that if you embrace the things that pertain to life and forsake the things that pertain to godliness, there are dimensions you will never experience and your growth process will not be complete. But there are others who will embrace the things that pertain to godliness and throw away the things that pertain to life, in the same way, you will not also have a balanced experience in your Christian walk, so it is expected that you gain understanding of the things that can bring you into the fullness of the things that pertain to life and the things that pertain to godliness; and Peter didn't leave us in the dark, he said these things are accessed

... through the knowledge of Him that hath called us unto glory and virtue, the knowledge is the key, the key is knowledge. But I summarize into three a thing that a Christian should know, a knowledge I believe a Christian should have a balance experience in his growth process in the kingdom

1, **The knowledge of God:** not necessarily the knowledge of principles first but the knowledge of the person of God, the person of His son Jesus Christ, the saving knowledge of Jesus. You need to understand who God is, the multi placated dimension of His operation, and the different possibilities that those dimensions can bring in men, there is a dimension of God as a father, what the dimension of God as a father produces is not the same as what the dimension of God as a king produces, so you need to know God in His different offices and His different dealings with man, you need to understand that God is all powerful, you need to understand that God is loving and always willing to do you good, you need to understand that every good and perfect gift comes from above from God the father of light in whom there is no variableness, neither there is shadow of turnings that means that if I see something that is not good, I can categorically say that this is not from God because I know the things that can come from God, I know what God is always doing, He's always willing to do good, He's able to do good, He's eager to do me good and He has everything that is needed to produce all the results and the possibilities that I desire in my life. You need to know God, you need to know that He is not one that won a competition among many gods, you need to know that His throne isn't threatened. When you read the Bible from Genesis to Revelation, there is never a time any man saw a revelation of Heaven and saw God standing, every time a man saw God, God was sitting, kings sit when there is rest, so there has never been a situation that warranted God being in an emergency standing mood, the only time we saw Him stand was when Jesus stood to receive Stephen, it was not because there was an emergency that He needed something to be done quickly to produce result. You need to understand that God is not scratching His head thinking of what to do with the earth, you need to know that God is not worrying saying eh! What is Satan doing? so the first knowledge you should have about God, are His omnipotence, His omnipresence, His omniscience, all-knowing, all-powerful, ever-present, able, willing, and eager to step into your matter. But after the knowledge of God, the knowledge of God in itself may not necessarily produce your result because yes you have understood the principles, there is another thing the knowledge of God should produce, He said; *who do men say that I am?* So, after saying so many things then Peter said; *Thou hath the Christ the son of the living God,* and then Jesus said; *flesh and blood has not revealed this to you but my father.* That means it is not given to a man to know what God is and who God is until God by Himself reveals that thing to that man, He said this is not revealed to you by flesh and blood, and I tell you the intent of this revelation; *I say unto you, because you recognize me as the Christ, the son of the living God, I say unto you, you are Peter, and upon this revelation of who you are, I will build my church.* I cannot build my church upon your knowledge of me, your knowledge of me should produce something about you that will be a foundation upon which I should build something. Your life is built on what you have discovered as your place in Christ, you need to understand our oneness in Him, you need to understand our position and advantage in Him, your knowledge of God must translate into a knowledge of you in God

2, **Satan**: I'm not trying to postulate a theory that we should start studying Satan, no, there are certain things you must know about Satan to remain victorious:

1.
   1. **The consequence of the cross upon him**: we know what the cross did for us, we know what the cross purchased for us, the cross did not only affect us, it's not just that it delivered us from the hands of Satan, there is something the cross did to Satan. When Satan hears the blood of Jesus, what comes to his mind? What does he think when you mention the name of Jesus? What effect did it have on him? What is Satan's current position relating to me? Where is Satan relative to me? If I'm addressing Satan, should I look up or down? Where is he? It's important you know where Satan is, relative to you.
   2. **Satan's strategies**: how many of you have ever wondered about what the bible has said about what we can accomplished when we are in Christ, we are a new creature, old things have passed away yet demons come to torment you, yet you know that what is happening to you is not a Godly spiritual process, it's entirely an activity of demonic forces. You are born again genuinely, you pray in tongues, anointed and even doing ministry, has it been a concern to anybody? It has been a concern to me and I

wonder if all power belongs to Jesus. Jesus said; *all powers in heaven, on earth, beneath the earth has been given to me.* I think Satan should belong to one of these three realms if he belongs to any of these three realms, that means whichever realm he belongs to, the power that is working with him should have been given to Jesus. How come Satan is still buffeting the life of people? What power is he using? And I realize that Satan is not necessarily using a power that is superior to what Jesus did, Satan is only strong to the degree that he can make his strategies secrets, the strength of Satan is his ability to hide in darkness, if his strategies are known he becomes powerless, they become powerless. The bible never instructed us to put on the whole armor of God to fight against the powers of Satan, He said to fight against the deceit, the wiles, that means the ability of Satan to deceive you is his greatest advantage

2 Corinthians 2 vs 11 Lest Satan should get an advantage of us: for we are not ignorant of his devices. The bible didn't say unless he takes advantage of us, it says lest he gets, that means if Satan succeeds in making you ignorant, the advantage is in his hand. It's not that he's trying to get it, the only thing Satan needs to do to have an advantage over your life, for a Christian to be in his hands is to receive you to be ignorant of his devices, Satan isn't so powerful

Ephesians 6 vs 11 Put on the whole armor of God, that ye may be able to stand against the wiles of the devil. The word 'wiles' there means deceit, the hidden strategies of the devil

Vs 12 For we wrestle not against flesh and blood, but against principalities, against powers, against the rulers of the darkness of this world, against spiritual wickedness in high places.

The living bible says; *put on all of God's armor so that you will be able to stand safe against all strategies and tricks of Satan, for we are not fighting against people made of flesh and blood but against persons without bodies, the evil rulers of the unseen world, those mighty satanic beings and great evil princes of darkness who rule this world and against huge numbers of wicked spirits in the spirit world.*

Men without bodies, people without bodies, he said so that we can stand against the strategies and the tricks of Satan. A believer who doesn't understands how Satan operates will be cheated by Satan and will be defeated by Satan, because what Satan is touching is not exactly where his interest is, it's a distraction because if you find out what he is doing, you will stop him, he knows that you have the power, the least of the saints can stop Satan, Yes! But his ability to shewed himself in darkness becomes the advantage he has over believers and Paul said; *all things are made manifest by the light.*

Isaiah 33 vs 22 For the LORD is our judge, the LORD is our lawgiver, the LORD is our king; he will save us

This is where the Americans got the concept of executive, legislature, and judiciary from. He said he shall save us, He will save us, the question is this, if He is going to save us, He's going to save us based on any of these three dimensions that is relevant for the bondage, it is not every time that He saves as king, it's not every time that He saves as judge, it's not every time that He saves as the lawgiver when the matter needs to be decided by a judge and you're praying to the Lord our king, He hears your prayers but that office doesn't carry the configuration to bring the result that you are looking for, because a judge does not veto a case, a judge decides a case by looking at the written code; your ability to present your case, your ability to defend whatever you are looking for, your ability to quote the presidency of the judicial process before the judge is what the judge will look at and will say that based on the evidences available before me, I give you justice. But a king doesn't need a judicial process, the bible says; *where the word of a king is, there is power.* So, you need to understand which dimension of God is responsible for producing the result.

At the time Isaiah wrote this, the nation of Israel has not gotten the revelation of God as a father, it was when Jesus was born that God was revealed as a father, so, that adds one to this; the Lord is our father, our judge, our lawgiver and our king. But the undoing of the body of Christ is that we are so much aware of God as a father that anytime we approach him, we are looking up to the father to give us justice, the father doesn't give justice, it is the judge that gives justice. The judge is the father; in this race, we are in if it has to do with the case of Satan, if you only know God as a father you will be limited. He is our father, but there is a limit to what His fatherhood can do. What did Job do to God? Is God not powerful again? Is He not the almighty? Is Satan not a creature that He created? Why couldn't he veto the demands of Satan? Why did He grant the demand of satan? God was the one that testified to satan; *have you considered my servant Job, he is perfect and eschewed evil and feareth the Lord.* Can God give a testimony of a man that is false? And Satan said; *I know that what you said about Job is true, but there is another thing I see, I'm approaching the court and there is a cross examination I want to do* and God was helpless. Do you think it was the desire of God for Job to go through what he went through? Why couldn't He stop satan? What makes you think He will stop satan?

God created man in a very unique way; Genesis 1 vs 26 -28

And God said, Let us make man in our image, after our likeness: and let them have dominion over the fish of the sea, and over the fowl of the air, and over the cattle, and over all the earth, and over every creeping thing that creepeth upon the earth.

So God created man in his [own] image, in the image of God created he him; male and female created he them

And God blessed them, and God said unto them, Be fruitful, and multiply, and replenish the earth, and subdue it: and have dominion over the fish of the sea, and over the fowl of the air, and over every living thing that moveth upon the earth

And the bible went on and told us how that God finished all He created. In chapter 2 vs 7 the bible began to give another account of the creation of man again, the bible said that God forms man out of the dust of the earth. He created man in His image, God is a spirit, and they that must worship Him, must worship Him in spirit and in truth, so if God made man in His image, it means man is a spirit and a spirit cannot function on earth without having a body, so God made a body for the man, the same thing He did with Jesus;... *a body as thou prepared me to do your will oh God.* The will is to be done on earth, then the spirit must have a body. And God made the body of man, the bible says ;.. *and God breath in the nostrils of that man and he became a living soul.* That means a soul compartment was given to the man, man became the only creature that has his unique configuration, he is a spirit and he is also physical, he can be in the realm of the spirit and earth at the same time, not even God could do that; uniquely designed, so man has the advantage of the realm of the spirit and of the earth and the soul given to man became the intermediary that interpreted the impulses of the spirit for the body to execute because the dominion has to be communicated in a language understood by the earth, the language spoken by the spirit cannot be understood by the earth so the soul becomes the intermediary that receives these impulses and interpreted it in a language that the earth can work with. God tested His creation to see how effective it is, the bible says God brought all the animals to man to see what he will name them and the bible says .. *whatever name Adam calls it, that was it.* That means the animals were named before they were brought to Adam but the information about the names was not revealed to Adam. Adam without consulting God named the animals, he called a lion, lion, and God said I called it Lion before I brought it to you, see the level of intelligence man operated in, until tragedy struck and the man fell and the man began to do guesswork, the bible says they made aprons of fig leaves and cover themselves and when God came, He made a coat of animal skin, imagine the difference in sophistication; fig leaves and coat. The man suddenly lost that intelligence because the God nature in him that made him reason like God had left, so from that time there was a desire in the heart of a mortal man to access the realm of the spirit because he knows that there is a possibility beyond human existence, so from that time, man was searching, they began to intercourse with all manner of wisdom, spirits and began to enter into certain covenant with them because the spirit cannot access the earth without an authorization by a man and the man is now limited because of his foe so there was a partnership between man and these spirits so that man can grant them authorization to come to the earth and these authorizations were made by what we call **ALTARS**; access points were created by men in an attempt to access the realm of the spirit. Interestingly, it is not only the Holy Spirit that can grant man access to the possibilities in the realm of the spirit, the spirit of dead men can also do that, the spirit of animals can also do it, that is why some people worship all kinds of animals. The Holy Spirit is not the only spirit that can activate spiritual realities in life of men, so men who are not willing to go back to God for the access, go to all these other diabolical temporary alternatives, because the process of accessing the wisdom that the Holy spirit brings requires that the man dies first because when God chased Adam out of the garden, the bible says that He placed at the entrance of the garden cherubim's and a flaming sword, the psalmist says where the cherubim's are that is where the throne of God is; when you see the simile to what He told Moses to build above the ark of covenant between the mercy seat where there are two cherubim that are covering it, He said between them are the throne of God, He said I will commune with you from above that point, so, the presence of the cherubim at the entrance of the garden means that God took His throne and place it at the entrance of the garden, the flaming sword there is Jesus Christ such that nobody can access the tree of life without first encountering the sword and when you meet the sword it must divide asunder, you can't go there and eat it as you are and men not willing to go through this process began to boycott and began to look for other spirits that can grant them access to this possibilities. This was the origin of witchcraft, we saw in Genesis 6 how that the sons (the fallen angels) of God saw the daughters of men that they were fair and they began to interact and intercourse with these daughters of men and sons were born into these falling spirits, and we saw that certain witchcraft divinations were on the face of the earth and evil began to increase. And in the days of Noah, God saw that Noah and his sons were perfect, that is they were the only pure humans not that there were sinless, they were the only pure human, others have interacted with fallen spirits and as a result of that had had their DNA compromised, they were no longer pure humans and God decided to destroy these people, but something happened very interestingly; God destroyed the people and preserved Noah and his three sons, their wives and Noah's wife, that means the only people that were preserved were the pure people, so where did evil come back from into the earth? All the evil men were destroyed but evil was still sustained. What exactly happened?

What is an altar?

An altar is a gateway between the realm of the spirit and the earth realm that grants unhindered access to certain spirit beings to find legal expression in the earth.

An altar is a legal landing spot of the spirit on the earth. An altar is an altar because of the presence of sacrifice, the realm of the spirit wants to interact with the realm of the earth legally and vice versa because the inhabitants of the earth knows that without the realm of the spirit they are limited in the possibilities that they can produce, they call for the assistance of these spirit beings. In agreement to bring these possibilities to the inhabitants of earth, the spirits give their conditions, certain things that can create a habitation that will look exactly like where they are coming from and then they summarize their demands in what they call **sacrifice** and they ask men to raise certain structures and put certain sacrifices. The kind of sacrifice on the altar depends on the kind of spirit that wants to access the earth, the absence of sacrifice on an altar makes it unqualified to be called an altar, thus, the sacrifice is what makes it an altar and the kind of spirit to whom the altar is raised determines whether the altar

THE MYSTERY OF ALTARS AND FOUNDATIONS

will be a good one or a bad one. Remember that the bible says we should present our bodies as living sacrifice, that means the minimum requirements to make the Holy Spirit come to the earth to assist you is that your body is your minimum requirement you can give to the Holy Spirit, so the same way different demon spirits have their demands as to the things that qualify to bring them to the earth. Some of the sacrifices are not necessarily animals, it can be certain abstinence from some things. Over time, we see that families and territories have activated altars, some unto God, others unto some spirits that give them momentary results for a while and suddenly begin to take some things from them. There is no spirit that assists any man without getting anything in return, including the Holy Spirit and what the Holy Spirit gets in return is you; every one of these, spirits their allegiance with you is not because of your commitment to them, it's because of the territory of the earth that is within your jurisdiction that you will bring under their control, it might just be one person who is looking for ends meet that invoked the spirit and thought he did it alone but the spirit is seeing that person's children, grandchildren, four and five generations from that person, the spirit knows it is just one person but if it can get him into the agreement, he knows how many people he is going to get, so many people are under influences of covenant that was entered by generations before they were born, they find themselves as Christians but are being driven by possibilities they can't explain because certain things were done.

Look at the life of Abraham, for example, the bible says that when God told Abraham to leave his father's house, and go to the land of Canaan, when God spoke with him, he raised an altar and he pitched his tent between Bethel where he raised an altar and Ai, and then left that place and went to Egypt, from Egypt he came back to where he raised his altar. Then, Abraham left the scene and Isaac came on board. One day Abraham's grandson Jacob was on his way to his uncle's house, then night fell and he decided to sleep, he was not trying to pray or seek God and it happened by divine orchestration, that he found himself lying down at the same spot where Abraham had raised an altar unto God. Suddenly, the bible says he had a dream and he saw a ladder ascending from the earth to heaven, angels ascending and descending. That portal didn't happen the day Jacob came there, from the day Abraham raised that altar, that gate was opened, from that day angels were ascending and descending and then the carrier of the covenant that Abraham enacted upon that altar came. Many people passed through that place, probably slept in that place, they didn't see that portal because when the covenant was entered, it was between Abraham and his seed so, you can come to that place, lie down and not see anything but if you are a seed of Abraham you must see. The moment Jacob came to that place, and lay down, suddenly the heavens were open and there was Yahweh standing, He said; I had a deal with Abraham in this place and there are certain things we agreed upon, one of those things is the land in which you lay, I will give it to you. Imagine if Abraham raised the altar unto a demonic spirit, Jacob will come there and still interact with the spirit because it was between Abraham and his seeds. Now, Jacob came to that place and had the experience, he stood up from that place and went to the house of Laban, labored for Rachel for 7years, labored for Leah for 7years, labored for Rachel another 7years and then worked for Laban for another 7years. As he was laboring there, in chapter 35, Jacob was dwelling where Shechem and his brothers were and because he understood that there was something about raising altar unto God, he raised an altar in that place and God said no, there is another altar that has been raised on your behalf, you don't have to raise another one, my dealings with you is based in the altar at Bethel and God said rise up and go to Bethel. And Jacob left with his family to Bethel, he activated that altar again and he called it El-Bethel.

Many years later, Israel came out of Egypt, they cross the Jordan, they brought down Jericho and they wanted to fight a little city called Ai and a man called Akan had taken something that does not belong to him and they couldn't defeat Ai. Then Joshua went to God and cried, what happened? Then God said Israel had sinned and they began to cast lot, got the person that did it, and cleansed the nation of that guilt. They went to war, lay ambush at a particular spot which was between Bethel and Ai, the same place Abraham built the altar, they never decided to go there but there was a force from the altar that is saying this land was given to Abraham and his seed, if you must take the land, you must align with the altar that Abraham had built and it was from that place they began to defeat all the nation.

Altars are trans-generational in their operation, they never die out with the person that erected it and it's amazing many of us are under the influence of one or more of these altars. Does it mean that the death of Jesus was in vain? No! But there is an intelligence you must have, you don't just get delivered from an altar by saying I don't want, there is a legal process that will break the altar. You don't wish your way out of the influence of an altar.

Negative altars have formed the foundation upon which many lives have been built, the reason behind the predicament, some sicknesses, troubles, failures that we see, they are altars that speak. The effects of these negative altars becomes stronger and more destructive by the next generation, you will be a wicked person not to pay attention to the altars that are around the family and the places where you come from, it is the peak of wickedness especially if you are a brother; altars are real, altars will stop you if you allow them. It is the integrity that supervises the operations of these altars, remember the Lord is our judge, lawgiver, and king.

There are many ways altars affect us, two of them are discussed below;

1, Territories: the places where we come from.

Mark 8 vs 22 and 23 *And he cometh to Bethsaida; and they bring a blind man unto him, and besought him to touch him.*

And he took the blind man by the hand, and led him out of the town; and when he had spit on his eyes, and put his hands upon him, he asked him if he saw. That means that as long as the man is in that territory, Jesus the son of the living God was limited in His ability to work miracle, Jesus held the hand of the man and as soon as they cross the boundary, the forces can no longer come there that is there are certain forces coming from territories produced in the life of people, you don't need to commit any sin or violate any law, the fact that you came from a particular place already implicated you. There is no city, village, Hamlet, that the first inhabitants did not enter a covenant with spirits before staying. Coming from a territory, blasting in tongues and a particular village is pulling you. When you observe the middle belt of Nigeria, their predicaments, limitations, and witchcraft is similar, it's not necessarily what the people did, there is something programmed into that territory, you didn't come from there doesn't exempt you from the impact. Haven't you noticed that there are some nations and cities in the bible, anytime God declares judgment on them you wonder what they did for example

Nineveh, what was their offense, the bible never told us what Nineveh did, God just asked Jonah to go and cry against Nineveh and when God changed His mind from destroying Nineveh, Jonah was angry, why? There was something Jonah knew about Nineveh that qualify them for destruction, but the king and his men exempted themselves from the judgment. It looked like God didn't destroy Nineveh but when you read the book of Nahum and Zephaniah, the judgment still happened.

How about Canaan? The Lord said Israel should wipe out everybody, what did they do? Idolatry? Israel did idolatry so it's not about what the Canaanites did? There is a long story

How about Babylon? Even till revelation, Babylon was still being punished.

Genesis 10; we said something about the generation of Noah earlier, Noah, his sons, and their wives, and Noah's wife were the eight people that were spared from the flood. But there is a story you need to read in between the lines to see;

Ham, the son of Noah was already interacting with those spirits, he didn't buy into their ideologies, he didn't participate in what they were doing but their mindset and ideologies were been sold to him. Ham was able to preserve their ideology from the pre-flood era to the post-flood era. It was based on this ideology Ham did something to his father, the bible called it seeing his father's nakedness. If you understand the speakings of scripture you will know that it is deeper than that, because Leviticus 20 vs 11 tells us that

Lev 20:11 And the man that lieth with his father's wife hath uncovered his father's nakedness: both of them shall surely be put to death; their blood [shall be] upon them.

So, it is not just about cloth been off, there are things that happened, the product of that thing that happened is Canaan and Noah said; *cursed be Canaan, a servant of servants shall he be unto his brethren..* So, Satan saw that Canaan had been cursed and he needs to preserve this and then he went after the first son of Ham called Cush. And the bible says that Cush gave birth to 4 sons in which their names were mentioned in *Genesis 10 vs 7 ; And the sons of Cush; Seba, Havilah, Sabtah, Raamah and Sabtecha: and the sons of Raamah; Sheba and Dedan.* When the bible says the sons of this person are these, that means at that time these are all the sons. But he didn't end there because none of these carried the ideology that Ham sustained, there was a need to find another person, then Cush had to give birth again, vs 8 says: *And Cush begat Nimrod; he began to be a mighty one in the earth. Vs 9: He was a mighty hunter before the Lord; wherefore it is said ...* The word before there means against and he became a reference point as Nimrod, the mighty hunter against the Lord. Nimrod became a standard for measuring rebellion and wickedness, so you are not rebellious enough until you are rebellious as Nimrod.

There was a preservation of the spirit of rebellion now finding expression in Nimrod and then we saw the things that happened in the life of Nimrod, the rebellion that he led that was all successful. It's like satan kept quiet for a while, he was watching, he saw that Shem begin to give birth such that Shem had a great grand-son called Terah and Terah had a son called Abraham and satan saw God entering a covenant with Abraham and that covenant by the understanding of satan is that there is a seed coming from here, because there is a prophecy in Genesis that the seed of the woman shall bruise his head, and he has been on the search and for the first time he heard God mentioning seed. *Leave your father's house to a land I will give you and to your seed after you.* So, satan said could this be the seed that God was talking about? And he began to follow that genealogy to see what he can do. And suddenly, the bible says Rebekah was pregnant and then there was trouble within her womb and she said *why I'm I like this?* and the Lord said *within your womb are two nations*, they are already fighting because of the agenda of darkness against the Christ, the firstborn fighting against the second born, and vice versa, but by God's ordination, *the elder shall serve the younger.* Then we saw how God said *Esau have I hated, Jacob have I loved.* Why will God hate a young man that was not born? Because the spirit of Nimrod was still hovering. The bible said they were born and grew up, Esau became a hunter. When you read Genesis 47 where the sons of Jacob came before Pharaoh and Pharaoh asked them their occupation, they said; *we and our fathers are shepherds.* Because they are the generation that should bring forth the Christ, that means their occupation must align with that, from who did Esau learn to be a hunter? It was the anti-Christ spirit that was already in Nimrod, and when God saw what Satan was going to do, He said if I allow Esau to carry the blessing, it means I am putting the Christ in an anti-Christ system. Now, Nimrod wasn't the direct father of Esau, but somehow, because they were cousins, it still found expression.

When you go back to Genesis 10 vs 10 *the beginning of his kingdom was Babel.* So, Babel didn't start in chapter 11, there was already a city that Nimrod had built, it was the tower that God confused; *And the beginning of his kingdom was Babel, and Erech, and Accad, and Calneh, in the land of Shinar.*

Daniel 1 vs 2 let's see where the land of Shinar is; *And the Lord gave Jehoiakim king of Judah into his hand, with part of the vessels of the house of God; which he (Nebuchadnezzar) carried into the land of Shinar to the house of his god....* King Nebuchadnezzar carried the vessels into a land that has been there before that time. Because the land of Shinar and kingdoms within it were built by Nimrod in rebellion against God, there is nothing they will ever do that will exempt them from the punishment of God, because the foundation was built on rebellion. It is not a question of whether Babylonians hate Israelites or not, they will have to die no matter how good they are. The blood of Jesus can only save the people but the land has to perish, because as far as God is concerned the land stands before God as a rebellious anti-Christ system that must be destroyed, why? Because of the man that built it.

Genesis 10 vs 11 *out of that land went forth Asshur (Assyria), and built Nineveh, and the city Rehoboth, and Calah.* Nimrod built Nineveh, that was why God said Nineveh should be destroyed. You see how the people at the time of Jonah were able to exempt themselves, they fasted and told God we have no part in this thing, we should not suffer for the things our fathers did and God said these people are sincere but I will still destroy this place but let me exempt this generation. When you read down in Genesis 10, you will see Canaan and the inhabitants of the place Canaan built, just by the way Canaan came, made him an enemy of God. Did you notice? The judgment of God upon Canaan was the exact judgment the flood did in the days of Noah. Destroy everybody, why will God say destroy everybody and will not say if you find a righteous person there? Because within this territory that originated from Canaan is Sodom and Gomorrah, all of these territories that God said they should destroy them completely, they were territories born based on this anti-Christ system of rebellion and God said there is no provision of repentance for them. In the same way, we come from many territories in this country built upon ancient traditions and altars that are speaking against us, the majorities of people are Christians but the altars are still there. You are doing the best you can, but there is a level you cannot go beyond. So, territories are mysteries that can produce realities in the life of people.

2, The mystery of tribes and ancestry:

Tribes are a very serious mystery in the realm of the spirit because while territories can be under the influence of certain covenant, there are individuals also that enter certain covenants. For example, Nimrod is an altar for everybody that came through his loins, Canaan himself already produced possibilities for everybody that came through his loins. Look at Moses, what stopped Moses from entering Canaan? The bible says that God told Moses to speak to the rock and Moses in anger because of the murmuring of the people, struck the rock and God said you haven't sanctified me before the people, look at the land but you will not enter it. Just anger? No! It's not just anger, because when you read Exodus 2 vs 1 the bible says; *a man of the house of Levi took to wife a daughter of Levi and the woman conceived and bare a son.* That was how the story of Moses began, that means the father and mother of Moses were Levites. Moses, a man that spent days in the presence of God, 40days the first and second time, stood before the bush, did all manner of things.

Genesis 49 vs 1: *And Jacob called unto his sons, and said, gather yourselves together, that I may tell you that which shall befall you in the last days.* He didn't say gather yourselves and your descendants, neither did he say gather yourselves with your wives and sons let me tell you what will happen, he said I'm going to be speaking to you as individuals.

Vs 2: *Gather yourselves together, and hear, ye sons of Jacob; and hearken unto Israel your father.*

Israel was the carrier of the covenant, remember that the name Israel was given to him after he encountered God. So, Jacob used that name as an invocation of his office as the current bearer of the Abrahamic covenant. In other words, what he is about to say will not fall to the ground.

Vs 5: *Simeon and Levi [are] brethren; instruments of cruelty [are in] their habitations.*

Vs 6: *O my soul, come not thou into their secret; unto their assembly, mine honour, be not thou united: for in their anger they slew a man, and in their selfwill they digged down a wall.*

Vs 7: *Cursed [be] their anger, for [it was] fierce; and their wrath, for it was cruel: I will divide them in Jacob, and scatter them in Israel.*

What stopped Moses from entering Canaan land? It was anger, it was said in vs 7. This was before they entered Egypt. So, before Moses was born, there was already a curse. I hope you know that the father of Moses was not the direct son of Jacob? He was not even the direct son of Levi; they might have forgotten those things. I hope you know it was Moses himself that wrote this? Cursed be their anger; cursed is the opposite of blessing. To bless means to empower to succeed, to curse means to empower to fail. Empowered to bring failure be their anger, Jacob said it and left it there. Years passed, they were giving birth. Moses' encounter with the burning bush removed leprosy but didn't remove this curse; his dwelling in the presence of God for 40days to a point that his face was glowing didn't remove this curse, his encounter with God the second time didn't remove this curse, his seeing the back of God didn't remove this curse, he was going to the presence of God with a curse and coming out of the presence of God with a curse, satan was not threatened by his encounters because there was something he had studied; Moses can be following God, do miracles in Egypt, but one day! Because satan was following Moses, the first time he tried to destroy him was through Pharaoh but it didn't work, then satan studied for 40years until one day he saw that Moses in anger killed an Egyptian and satan said this anger isn't ordinary and he saw that there was something Jacob placed upon the anger of his ancestors and he said let me explore this. Moses did it the first time when he saw the Golden calf, he was angry and he broke the commandments, God didn't kill him, he went further to grind the Golden calf and gave Israel to drink, satan said we are close until he got to that point.

Another person is David. Do you think that the adultery David committed was his love for women? No! David was not a product of legitimate birth, he said it in Psalm 51: *I was sharpened in iniquity, in sin did my mother conceive me.* It was because of the stories surrounding his birth that Jesse didn't consider him qualified, because according to the law of Moses, anybody that is born out of a relationship that is not legally marital, is considered a bastard and the bible says *the bastard shall not come into the congregation of the Lord, even unto his tenth generations shall he not come.* So, when Samuel came and said bring your sons, Jesse brought the ones that were legally born and left the one that was illegally born. David love God, killed Goliath, sang Psalms, yet this thing was there, it wasn't afraid of his worship, singing to God, it was still there following him, until the day it happened, that was not the first time David started liking a man's wife, Bathsheba was not the first married woman David was eyeing. The bible said when Nabal died, David went and married Abigail, at what point did David started nursing a desire for Abigail? The day Nabal died? It just happened that at that time he didn't have a supreme power that he can kill and do anything, there was a curse. When you study the family of David, you will see that there are marital messes that were there. the members of David's army, sons of David's elder sister, Zeruiah. It is in the character of scripture to name people by their father's name, but when you read through your bible you will never see anywhere that the name of the fathers of these boys was called, you will always see the sons of Zeruiah, a woman. It is either possible that they have different fathers or the name of their father was not known.

Judah gave birth to three sons, the first one was wicked before God, God killed him, the second son, the same thing, the third one was growing and Judah refuses to give to Tamar to marry, and Tamar disguised herself as a harlot and Judah slept with her. Judah patronizes harlots and Judah was the ancestor of David, so it is normal for Judah to visit harlots. It happened that Judah didn't have money to pay cash, so he gave the harlot his scepter, the symbol of his authority. Then, after some days he sent his friend to go and deliver the price and his friend came there he didn't find the harlot. After sometime Tamar became pregnant, according to the law she should be stoned because she had committed adultery then she brought out the scepter and said the owner of this authority is responsible, so Judah got his son's wife pregnant. Judah's sister, Diana was raped. David's daughter, Tamar, because there was two curses speaking, the curse of rape and womanizing, so Amnon took the father's dimension and Tamar fell victim of the mother's dimension, nothing just happens. These are men that represents a strange dimension in God, if they were not exempted, there must be something you must know that will free you. Men don't just access freedom by desire, there is something you must know. Territories can bring somebody under an influence so also tribes too, you don't have to do anything.

The question is this, has God left us without hope? No, He hasn't. There is a bailout plan, but before we discuss the bail plan, let's see what satan does with this information to destroy us. Remember the life of Job, Satan came to God that there is something I've seen, give me permission. Where was that conversation happening? Because satan has been driven from heaven, from the presence of God, so, at what point was he meeting with God to do this conversation? If satan was not qualified to come to the presence of God, to the house of God, where is he meeting God? He is meeting God in court. My father is a judge right? That He disowns me as been member of the family does not mean I cannot come to the court where he is a judge, the court is an institution that grants everybody access to present his case so satan has the right to come to the court of God. Revelation 12 vs 10 tells us that the accuser of the brethren has been cast down. What does he do? He accuses our brethren, that means that as we are here, there are reports going on in heaven, who is bringing the reports? Satan! What are the reports? This person is from this territory and based on the records, these are the things about that territory and because of this he can't progress. See where our fathers missed it, they were born in this circumstances in that territorial or ancestral curse and then they met the missionaries who preached the gospel to them, and they told them to give their life to Christ and be saved and they innocently gave their lives to Christ and they were saved. They didn't understand the differences between prophetic realities and the experience of it. For instance, my father is late and left a portion of land with the documents, my possessing those documents does not mean somebody can't wake up one day and says it's his land, he can start building on that land and I show him the documents of the land to prove to him he isn't the owner of the land, such person can kill me and collect the papers, what then do you do, you take those papers to the court of competent jurisdiction and tell them someone is trespassing your land, then the court will summon the person and ask him or her to present the evidence that the land belongs to him, the court will weigh both pieces of evidence and declare the first person as the owner. Then, the court will provide law enforcement agencies, so that anytime the man is found in the land again, he will be chased.

So, we gave our lives to Christ, got the certificate of birth and evidence of our inheritance yet satan is still moving in our land and all we are doing is get out, you think he'll go? No! It is only a court process that will give you the justice. He accuses us before God day and night but vs 11 *And they overs came him by the blood of the lamb, and by the word of their testimony; and they loved not their lives unto death.* What exactly happened? What is John saying? What did John see here?

Revelations 5 vs 9 *And they sung a new song, saying, Thou art worthy to take the book, and to open the seals thereof: for thou wast slain, and hast redeemed us to God by thy blood out of every kindred, and tongue, and people, and nation.* Who are the 'they' singing a new song? The elders, remember that John was weeping that there was none in heaven or in the earth that could take the book or lose the seals thereof and one of the 24 elders came to John and said weep no more for the lion of the tribe of Judah has prevailed and the moment the elders said that, they began to sing. Remember we said an altar is called altar because of the presence of sacrifice and the value of the sacrifice upon the altar determines the strength of the voice of that altar, so, if an altar is erected against me, I will need a sacrifice that is higher than the one that was used to invoke that altar to undo that. There are altars upon territories, families and these altars were built on sacrifices but here is another sacrifice. The validity of sacrifice is the age of that sacrifice, but this sacrifice here is God Himself, ageless. His blood was a business process, Jesus purchased men unto God from every tribe, if your tribe is still asking for payment you can go to court. He purchased men unto God from every tribe, languages, people, nations. Nation talks about territories, so this is what the blood of Jesus did, we know this, yet there is still battle. The tribes, languages, people, and nations have been paid in full but still say I belong to them, which means I should go to court. But, there is a standard process in the court of God, you can't just walk to God anyhow, there are accredited people.

1st John 5 vs 7: *For there are three that bear record in heaven, the Father, the Word, and the Holy Ghost: and these three are one.* That means that there are three offices but the same person

Vs 8: *And there are three that bear witness in earth, the Spirit, and the water, and the blood: and these three agree in one.* The spirit has all the stories, he bears records and witness, the bible didn't say these three are one, they agree in one. That means the voice of the spirit is different from the voice of the water, and also is different from the voice of the blood. The voice of the water is saying in Ephesians 5, Paul said *.. that he might sanctify and cleanse it with the washing of water by the word.* That means it's the sanctifying dimension of the word of God. The blood-bought you, the water declares your sanctification but there must be an agreement of three witnesses before the inheritance can be given to you. Man is the one not progressing, been limited, not getting a job but man is not an accredited witness, the spirit the water and the blood. Acts 1 vs 8 says that *but ye shall receive power, after that the Holy Ghost is come upon you..* The same spirit who is an accredited witness come upon you and you shall be witnesses unto me. As a man, you are not accredited, but in partnership with the Holy Spirit, the slot of the Holy Spirit becomes your slot. Unlike Job who wasn't present when his matter was been discussed. Ephesians 1 vs 13 the Holy Ghost is the seal of our redemption, a seal is an authentication that means the blood purchase redemption, the Holy Ghost authenticates redemption, the Holy Ghost is a matter of life and death, it doesn't just help you to pray in tongues alone, when there is a summon in the court of heaven, there is a cross-examination, you're praying to move forward and then Satan brings his accusations, the blood is saying I paid, the water is saying I sanctified and then Satan will say let me cross-examine him, then it begins and suddenly troubles began, everyone starts provoking you, businesses begin to fail, everything is hitting you and the bible says the attempt is to make Job sin with his mouth, not just to lose everything, if he says something different from what the blood and water are saying he will lose his case in court and but for us the Holy Ghost is with us here on earth, Jesus the advocate is with the father. When you are getting tired to pray, the Holy Spirit says no, keep praying, the case is still in the court, at a point the Holy Spirit asks you to start dancing, it looks as if what your doing isn't making sense. **What are you tired about? take the matter to court.**

Prayers

1. I challenge every altar in my family that supervises my life, by the blood of Jesus I exempt myself.
2. Satan, enough is enough, I am a Christian and I am born again, the blood of Jesus purchased me, therefore it is wrong for you to withhold my inheritance based on my ancestry, I've been bought with a price.

Declaration

In the name of Jesus, I declare that I am born again and the implication of that is I have been bought with a price out of every tribes, languages, people, and nation, country, family, tongue, and territories, I've been crucified with Christ, I am a brand new person, therefore, I declare by the blood of Jesus that every affliction, sickness, delay, failures, stagnations, misfortune, in my life, the curse of ancestries, territories, I declare by the blood of Jesus that it is illegal, therefore I appear before the court of heaven to demand restoration now. I have taken my finances, my health, my marriage, my career, my relationship back in Jesus name.

http://amazon.com/author/apostlejoshuaselman

- **PRAYER POINTS.**
1, Thank God for the privilege He has given you to be alive till this moment
2. If you are born again, thank God for the salvation of your soul, if not make confession unto
salvation according to Romans 10:10.
3. Plead the blood of Jesus upon yourself and your loved ones.
Pray the following with utmost concentration and focus:
4. My heavenly clouds full of rain of blessings release them now in Jesus name.
5. I reject failure at the edge of success this season in Jesus name.
6. My glory will not collapse nor cut off in Jesus name.
7. Powers that may want to introduce failure and delay into my life and career be arrested in
Jesus name.
8. Any contrary wind that may want to blow against my progress fade away in Jesus name.
9. Any veil covering the manifestation of my glory, I set you on fire in Jesus name.
10. Every limitation imposed by dark power upon my breakthrough this year be broken in
Jesus name.
11. Every embargo of darkness on my glory be lifted by fire in Jesus name.
12. Oh Lord deliver me from mistakes that can hinder my blessings.

13. Wherever I am expecting a positive answer, I reject a negative answer and response in Jesus name.
14. All my divine helpers shall locate me and help me in Jesus name.

- Praise God for His mercies over your life.
- Repent of all sins and iniquities that can deprive of God's favour and mercies
- Father, help me to be rightly positioned for the flow of your blessings and deliverance.
- Lord, let there always be cry of GRACE, MERCIES and FAVOUR in my home, business and my life.
- I reject, refuse, resist anything in my family, business, home, life, resisting the favour of God in Jesus name.
- Wherever I go for the rest of this year, the light of God's deliverance and blessings will shine around me in Jesus name.
- Lord, let your deliverance power silence every opposition in my life in Jesus name.
- Lord, Let your current of favour flow into my life in Jesus name.
- All my helpers assigned to me by God will locate me this year in Jesus name.
- By the favour of God I shall testify and praise God in Jesus name.
- You are greatly BLESSED!

1. I command every spiritual abnormality in my life to be terminated in the name of Jesus.
2. By your cleansing blood, wash and flush out every dirt in my spiritual pipe.
3. Every stubborn mountain in my life, be removed in Jesus' name.
4. I command every power oppressing me to be roasted, in the name of Jesus.
5. I command every hindrance to my breakthrough to be

THE MYSTERY OF ALTARS AND FOUNDATIONS

removed, in the name of Jesus.

6. I command loophole in my spiritual life through which the enemies is afflicting me to be closed forever in the name of Jesus.
7. Father, by your mighty hand, repair evrything the devil have damaged in my life Jesus' name.
8. I declare that i shall succeed in life and no devil can stop it in the name of Jesus.
9. I cover myself with the blood of jesus, in Jesus' name.
10. I confess that my life shall be full of breakthrough testimonies in the name of Jesus.
11. Every evil padlock and every evil chain against my breakthrough go back to the senders, in the name of Jesus.
12. I rebuke every spirit of deafness and blindness in my life, in the name of Jesus.
13. I bind the strongman behind my breakthrough and paralyse his operations in my life, in Jesus' name.
14. I anoint my eyes and my ears with the blood of Jesus.
15. O Lord, restore my spiritual eyes and ears, in the name of Jesus.
16. Lord, anoint my eyes and my ears that they may see and hear you clearly in Jesus name
17. I melt away any satanic deposits, resisting my breakthrough in the name of Jesus.
18. Spiritual eyes and ears, I command you in the name of Jesus, be opened.
19. In the name of Jesus, I capture every power behind every form of backwardness in my life in Jesus name
20. I declare that i have a sound mind, therefore i shall succeed in life in the name of Jesus
21. I reject the spirit of poverty in Jesus name

22. I reject the spirit of mediocrity in Jesus name
23. I reject the spirit of failure in Jesus name
24. I reject the spirit of back wardness in Jesus name
25. I reject the spirit of laziness in Jesus name
26. I reject the spirit of near success syndrome in Jesus name
27. I reject the spirit of delays in Jesus name
28. I reject the spirit of lack and want in Jesus name
29. I reject the spirit of ups and downs in Jesus name
30. I reject the spirit of bad luck and hard luck in Jesus name.
31. I declare that I have a sound mind, therefore I will excel in life in Jesus name
32. I declare that I shall have good success in my life in Jesus name
33. I declare that no matter where I maybe now, I shall get to the top in Jesus name.
34. I declare that I shall rise from this dust to the throne in Jesus name
35. I may be a nobody now, but in no distant time my God will make me a global celebrity in Jesus name
36. I declare that I shall always be the head and not the tail in life
37. The spirit of wisdom is at work in me in Jesus name
38. The spirit of understanding is at work in me in Jesus name
39. The spirit of boldness is at work in me in Jesus name
40. The spirit of humility is at work in me in Jesus name.
41. I stand against every wall of Jericho standing between me and my breakthrough in Jesus name.
42. I subdue all resistant forces fighting me and my break-

through in Jesus name
43. I decree eternal calamity upon every evil man or woman fighting my breakthrough
44. By the power of God, I scatter every conspiracy of hell against my life in Jesus name
45. By the power of the holy spirit, I destroy every enchantments against my break through in Jesus name.
46. Every secret enemy fighting my breakthroughs, I expose you and humiliate you forever in Jesus name.
47. Every monitoring spirit monitoring my breakthrough, go blind now in Jesus name
48. Let the hand of God break the back bone of every evil strongman on my way in Jesus name.
49. I return to the sender, every evil utterance against my life and destiny in Jesus name.
50. Father thank you for answering my prayers in Jesus name.

PRAYER POINTS.
- Thank God for the Gift of Life for you and your family.
- If you are born again, thank God for the salvation of your soul; if not make confession unto salvation according to Romans 10:10.
- Plead the blood of Jesus upon yourself and your loved ones.
-
- Pray the following with utmost concentration and focus:
- My heavenly clouds full of rain of blessings release them now in Jesus name.
- I reject failure at the edge of success this season in Jesus name.
- My glory will not collapse nor cut off in Jesus name.
- Powers that may want to introduce failure and delay

into my life and career, be arrested in Jesus name.
- Any contrary wind that may want to blow against my progress fade away in Jesus name.
- Any veil covering the manifestation of my glory, I set you on fire in Jesus name.
- Every limitation imposed by dark powers upon my breakthrough be broken in Jesus name.
- Every embargo of darkness on my glory be lifted by fire in Jesus name.
- Oh Lord, deliver me from mistakes that can hinder my blessings.
- Wherever I am expecting positive answers, I reject negative answers and responses in Jesus name.
- All my divine helpers shall locate me and help me in Jesus name.

- **PROPHETIC DECLARATION.**
- Declare loud and clear to yourself;
- - Any evil power/spirit/personality visiting me at night in my dreams or sent to me from hell in order to .....ABORT MY BREAKTHROUGH....be arrested in Jesus name.
- - Any evil power/spirit/personality visiting me at night in my dreams or sent to me from hell in order to ....PLANT SICKNESS IN MY BODY.... be arrested in Jesus name.
- - Any evil power/spirit/personality visiting me at night in my dreams or sent to me from hell in order to ....POLLUTE ME & MY DESTINY.... be arrested in Jesus name.
- - Any evil power/spirit/personality visiting me at night in my dreams or sent to me from hell in order to ....STEAL MY GOODNESS AND REMOVE FAVOUR FROM MY LIFE.... be arrested in Jesus name.
- - Any evil power/spirit/personality visiting me at night in my dreams or sent to me from hell in order to ....NAKED MY GLORY, CAUSE DELAY, STAGNATION AND FRUSTRATION.... be arrested in Jesus name.

About The Apostle

Apostle Joshua Selman Apostle Joshua Selman Nimmak – an anointed minister and revelational teacher of the Word of God. He is founder/leader of Eternity Network International (ENI) and convener of Koinonia – a weekly programme where people come to experience WORSHIP, WORD, MIRACLES AND LOVE, experience true intimacy with the Holy spirit and learn to be with Him, be like Him and represent Him.

Made in United States
North Haven, CT
02 December 2022